Luxembourg Travel Guide

Sightseeing, Hotel, Restaurant
& Shopping Highlights

Thomas Austin

Table of Contents

Luxembourg

The small European nation of Luxembourg is home to many leading European Union (EU) agencies and institutions. The European Investment Bank, European Court of Justice, General Court and the Court of Auditors are located here as are some of the departments of the European Commission. Luxembourg is one of the three Benelux states along with Belgium and the Netherlands and is a member of the United Nations.

The EU has seven major institutions in the cities of Brussels, Frankfurt, Strasbourg and Luxembourg. The EU started life as the European Coal and Steel Community (ECSC) in 1951 and Luxembourg was one of the original members. Prior to this is 1949 Luxembourg became a charter member of the North Atlantic Treaty Organization (NATO) and in 1961 joined the Organisation for Economic Cooperation and Development (OECD).

In October 2012 Luxembourg was elected to serve on the United Nations Security Council for the first time, being the only EU non-permanent member at the time.

For much of its history Luxembourg was dominated by other European nations and its independence and neutrality wasn't recognised until 1867. The status of Grand Duchy was granted in June 1815 by the Congress of Vienna and political autonomy was granted in 1839 by King William I of the Netherlands. He was also the Grand Duke of Luxembourg.

The country has two distinct parts; the northern third has the high plateau of the Ardennes while the other two thirds are made up of broad valleys and undulating countryside of Gutland. The south with its fertile soil is wonderfully rich and many soft fruits are produced here.

A 25-mile stretch of the Moselle river forms a natural border with Germany and there are several minor rivers that criss-cross the country. Plenty of water coupled with lush valleys and thickly forested areas means there is no shortage of fresh food.

Luxembourg has more Michelin-starred restaurants per capita than anywhere in the world and their chefs take full advantage of the locally produced foods. Speciality dishes with fresh trout and pike feature on many menus as do Ardennes ham and jugged hare. The capital is a gourmet food lover's paradise with many vibrant and bustling restaurants to choose from.

One dish that is served everywhere in various forms and to various standards is tartare. Tartare is a mixture of finely chopped or minced raw meat or fish; some of the most common being venison, beef, horsemeat, salmon or tuna. A variety of herbs and seasonings are added and served on a slice of rye bread, sometimes with a raw egg on top. For the less adventurous there are cafes everywhere serving impressive chocolates and pastries.

All those calories mean that some form of exercise will be needed and what could be better than a stroll round this historic city where modern living nestles side by side with elegant buildings from the past. There are many contrasts to be found and a good way to make sure that nothing is missed is to follow the excellent Wenzel's Walk.

Walking, talking and taking photos can be thirsty work and Place d'Armes is a great place to enjoy a coffee or a chilled glass of Moselle wine. After quenching your thirst find the Chemin de la Corniche which is frequently called the most beautiful balcony in Europe. The promenade overlooks the Alzette river and the Grund (lower town) and stretches away across the rooftops and valleys to the tall buildings of Kirchberg and the financial district in the distance. If nightlife is what you are after there is some good places around the Chemin de la Corniche for partying and dancing.

Situated about ten miles from the capital is the spa town of Montdorf-les-Bains. The thermal spa is ideal for relaxation and rejuvenation after a hard days sightseeing and some lava stone therapy and an algae wrap will have you raring to go in no time at all. The richly mineralised waters stay at a pleasant 24°C and are said to help with liver, gastric and respiratory ailments. After all this luxury treatment you might need to try and recoup some cash and conveniently the only casino in Luxembourg is close by.

For active holidays in the Grand Duchy, the Upper Sûre Nature Park with its beautiful lake and stunning scenery is the place to go. Kayaking, water skiing and sailing are available and there are plenty of hiking trails and scenic places to picnic and enjoy the peaceful surroundings. There is a strong local craft industry and many beautiful items can be purchased. Look out for the earthenware whistles shaped like birds. These Peckvillercher birds were traditionally exchanged between lovers but are very popular now at any festival or celebration especially Emaischen on Easter Monday.

There are 30 designated cycle routes and it is possible to travel from north to south across the whole country without even sharing the road with a car.

Culture

It is a wonder the Luxembourgers ever sleep as there is usually a festival, procession or musical event happening somewhere. The hectic schedule includes the ING Marathon, the October Nuts Market, Rock-A-Field and the Festival of Wiltz to name just a few. Luxembourg is a wonderful country for music lovers with many of the events throughout the year. From classical to clubbing and heavy rock to harmonies there is plenty to choose from.

In early March the Printemps Festival begins and continues until early June. Held in the capital (Luxembourg) this festival features international and local artists and is used as a platform for new talent. All across the capital various productions take place; for clubbing and live concerts head to Den Atlier or for something easier on the ears try the Grand Théâtre de Luxembourg.

East of the capital, the Echternach Music Festival is held in May and June. This international event has played host to such famous names as Yehudi Menuhin and Dietrich Fischer-Dieskau who take to the stage with up and coming local talent. The performances take place in the churches of St Peter and Paul and St Willibrord and classical as well as modern compositions are played.

Echternach is also home to a rather curious hopping procession. Every year on Whit Tuesday around 10,000 people hop, skip and dance though the town to a lively polka tune played by a marching band. The participants can only wear plain trousers and white tops, no fancy dress or traditional costumes are allowed, and they wave white handkerchiefs as they gaily dance past. The event is in honour of St Willibrord, the patron saint of Luxembourg.

As the warmer summer months approach the Luxembourgers celebrate their national holiday on 23rd June held in honour of Grand Duchess Charlotte (1919-1964). She was actually born on 23rd December but as winter is never the best time for birthday parties the celebrations were changed to June 23. Through the day the Grand Duke inspects the military parade on the Avenue de la Liberté and then the royal party visits Luxembourg Cathedral where they take part in singing the Te Deum, an early Christian hymn of praise, accompanied by much pomp and ceremony.

In the evening thousands of people line the streets to watch the torch-lit parade and they cheer the royal family before proceeding to the Adolphe bridge to watch the firework display. Later it's party time with live music and entertainment in many of the capital's squares.

Many individual and team sports take place in Luxembourg. Football is the top sport and the first national game was played in 1913. The team, nicknamed the Lions, is not particularly strong and since 2002 has never ranked above 150th in the world!

For three weeks in August the Schueberfouer fair brings the capital of Luxembourg to life. It was originally a cattle and flea market that started in 1340 but todays fair is of a different kind; much bigger, noisier and glitzier. The gentle lowing of cattle and strumming of lutes has long been replaced. Nowadays it is the screaming of youngsters as they whizz round on death defying rides to the thumping sound of music played at many decibels over the legal limit.

The fair lasts for eight days and as well as thrilling rides there are a number of market stalls selling anything from roasted hazelnuts to bargain CD's and kitchen items. The fair is located on the Glacis car park in the Limpertsberg district and the Ferris wheel and roller coasters can be seen from afar, as well as the music heard. As with any fair there are food and drink stalls to tempt the taste buds. One of the specialities is Fouerfësch, whiting fried in brewer's yeast, served with chips and washed down with a tankard of locally brewed beer or glass of dry Moselle wine.

Location & Orientation

Luxembourg is one of the smallest nations in the world at 998 square miles and is completely landlocked. It is surrounded by Germany, France and Belgium and is the only remaining grand duchy. The current duke is Henri, Grand Duke of Luxembourg and Duke of Nassau. He became head of the country in October 2000 after the abdication of his father.

Officially called the Grand Duchy of Luxembourg the country has two main regions; Oesling in the north and Gutland in the south. These are divided into 3 districts, sub-divided into 12 cantons and finally into 106 communes. The capital is Luxembourg City.

As would be expected many of Luxembourg's culture and traditions are closely influenced by the neighbouring countries and the official language is the same. Luxembourgish is a mixture of German and French with some Dutch thrown in. Children at infant school learn Luxembourgish first; primary school education is in French and secondary school education in German.

Residents need all the language skills they can get as the official language of the parliament, law and civil service is French, court cases and parliamentary debates are in Luxembourgish and police records and the media is in German. Many people expand their linguistic skills by learning English and Dutch as well.

The economy in Luxembourg is strong and this has attracted many foreigners to enjoy the high wages and low taxes. Nearly half of the population of 524,000 are not Luxembourgers and there are estimated to be 150 different nationalities living in the country. Employment in the country is mainly provided by EU, government as well as banking, insurance and technology jobs.

The country is (somewhat controversially) the world headquarters for Skype and the European headquarters of both Paypal and Amazon. It is also home to RTL Group (Radio Télévision Luxembourg) the largest TV, radio and production company in Europe. Luxembourg is the country responsible for many people round the world receiving satellite television as in 1981 the communications company, SES, launched the first Astra satellite. Now around 74 million homes worldwide receive broadcasts from Astra and other subsequent satellites.

Luxembourgers have much to celebrate. The country has one of the lowest unemployment rates in Europe and has the second highest minimum wage in the world after Australia. There are 155 banks and Luxembourg is a well-known tax haven.

The transport infrastructure in Luxembourg is excellent. Findel Airport is the only international airport in the country and is conveniently located a few miles from the capital. There are direct flights to all the major European airports plus the Canary Islands, Morocco, Tunisia, Turkey and Egypt. Connections to the city centre are available by bus or taxi. There are plans for a train station to be built at the airport in the future.

The train station in Luxembourg City is easily accessible and the main building is built from warm honey-coloured stone and is very pretty when lit up at night. The Baroque Revival style building is a far cry from the all steel and glass construction of so many train stations these days and the imposing clock tower can be seen for miles around. The station serves as the hub for the entire domestic and international railway network apart from Line 80 and high-speed trains connect Luxembourg to Germany, France and Belgium.

Luxembourg has a network of well-planned roads and getting around the country is easy as it only measures 51 miles north to south and 35 miles east to west. Parking can be an issue, especially in Luxembourg City at weekends so although car parks are well signposted sometimes the bus might be the better choice.

The city centre bus service is efficient and reliable and connects all the major parts of the city and suburbs as well as the airport. Every village in the country has a bus service with an hourly service on weekdays. Bus tickets can be bought from the driver and cost €1.50 for travel within two hours of purchase or €4 for the whole day. The same ticket is valid on the trains.

As Luxembourg is mostly flat many people take advantage of the 360 miles of cycle paths and there are a variety of routes around the country. Cycle rental is available at many locations and for casual users a cycle can be hired for the day at Veloh in Luxembourg City and Vel'OK in Eisch-sur-Alzette.

Climate & When to Visit

Luxembourg experiences warm summers but there is no particularly dry season as the mild temperate climate means there are many damp days. The middle of December is the most likely time for rain but there is a pretty good chance of rain whatever month it is.

The summer season is short; from 1st June to September 6th with an average of 19°C. The hottest period is early August when highs of 23°C can be reached with a low of 14°C. The third week of June sees nearly 17 hours of daylight per day, however, the same month is more likely to bring thunderstorms.

Winter is from November 14th to March 4th and the mercury only reaches a rather chilly daytime high of 7°C. The shortest day with 8 hours of daylight is on 21st December and the weeks either side of this date are generally cold, damp and gloomy. Everyone hurries about their business huddled up in thick coats, scarves and waterproof footwear. The coldest times are in January with an average low of -1°C and there is a good chance of snow.

Late spring and early autumn are perhaps the nicest times to visit, with daylight until around 10pm whereas in the winter it is dark by 4pm. The temperatures in both seasons is similar with maybe a few degrees colder in the spring, a high of 12°C is about average with the low being just above freezing.

Everywhere is less crowded out of the main seasons and prices are usually slightly cheaper as well. Some attractions and venues do close through the less popular months so be sure to check well ahead to avoid disappointment. Whatever time of year you choose to visit it might be advisable to pack a variety of clothes to cope with all weathers and keep an umbrella handy.

Sightseeing Highlights

Wenzel Walk (1,000 Years in 100 Minutes)

Meeting point:
Luxembourg City Tourist Office
Place Guillame II
L-2011 Luxembourg City
Tel: +352 222 809
www.lcto.lu

This walking tour is a really super way to see the best parts of Luxembourg City and learn about its history. Departing from the tourist office the tour takes approximately two hours and takes in the Bock Casemates, the Chemin de la Corniche, the Wenzel Ring Wall, the Old Gates and ends in the Alzette valley.

It was Wenceslas II, the Duke of Luxembourg who fortified the city and this is where the route gets its name from. Many of the old fortifications can be seen as the tour winds through the town crossing many of the medieval bridges.

The tour takes place on Wednesday and Saturday at 3pm and is a guided tour. The guides speak English, French and German and are always happy to answer any questions about their beautiful city. Reservations can be made in advance online or in person at the tourist office. The price is €10 for adults, €8 for students and senior citizens and €5 for children.

Bock & Petrusse Casemates

Bock Casemates

Montée de Clausen
L1343- Luxembourg City
Tel: +352 222 809
www.lcto.lu/

Petrusse Casemates

Place de la Constitution
Bd F.D. Roosevelt
L-2450 Luxembourg City
Tel: +352 222 809
www.lcto.lu/

The Casemates are the biggest tourist attraction in
Luxembourg City with 100,000 visitors each year. In 1994
UNESCO added the Casemates to the World Heritage
List as this maze of tunnels is such an important example
of a defence system.

During a period of domination by the Spanish in 1644 the
first tunnels were excavated and then 40 years later
enlarged by a French military engineer, the rather
impressively named Sébastien Le Prestre maréchal de
Vauban. In the 18th century the Austrians took their turn
at adding to the different levels and depths of the
passageways, some as far down as 130 feet. The
Casemates have been called the Gibraltar of the North as
there is a striking similarity between the caves and
tunnels in both places.

The tunnels were originally 14 miles in length but after
the fortress was dismantled in 1867 about 10 miles were
left and these are longest tunnels in the world. The
Casemates were first opened to the public in 1933 and
have seen thousands of feet pass through in the
intervening years. Guided tours depart every hour and
opening times are daily from 10am to 5pm. Admission
price is €3 per adult and €2.50 for children.

Trinitarian Church, Vianden

Grand-rue
L-9411 Vianden
Luxembourg
Tel: +352 2695 0566

The Trinitarians built this fine example of Gothic art in 1248 after they had been summoned to Vianden by Count Henry I. A devastating fire destroyed most of the church in 1498 but rebuilding and restoration work was carried out and several additions made through the years. The choir was added in 1644 and in 1693 the organ was installed.

Above the entrance portal there is a beautiful 14th century statue representing the Virgin Mary and Child and adjoining the church is the Cloister with its pleasant and serene gardens. In the Cloister there is a small lapidary museum.

The church is unusual as it has two altars and two naves. The main altar is quite stunning and was built in 1758. Two Vianden artists, Daleyden and Goldschmit, were responsible for building this rather ornate and gilded masterpiece. The other altar dates back to the 15th century and comes from the workshop of Rupert Hoffman of Trier. Care of the naves was divided and the right nave was looked after by the monks while the left nave was left to the parishioners.

In 1988 numerous tombs were discovered and the floor was lowered about 18 inches to take it back to its original level.

Vianden Castle & Chairlift

Vianden Castle

Vianden
Luxembourg
Tel: +352 8341 081
www.castle-vianden.lu/

It would be quite hard to miss the castle on a visit to Vianden as it sits high above the town against a back drop of thick forest. In 1820 the castle was sold off piece by piece by King William of Holland and subsequently fell to rack and ruin. Eventually the ownership was transferred from the Grand Duke of Luxembourg to the State and Vianden Castle stared the long road to recovery.

This comprehensive restoration of the castle took place in 1977 and ever since then it has been a must-see tourist attraction in Luxembourg. The castle website has some excellent photos of the castle before and during the restoration.

Not all of the rooms have been completely restored, some leave a little bit to the imagination and there are 20 different rooms that can be seen as the visitor route passes through the castle. The kitchen is amazing and gives a real insight into what it would have like to live and work in the castle without all of today's modern conveniences. In one of the bedchambers, an ornately carved four-poster bed with thick red curtains takes pride of place. The huge fireplace and warming pan would have been essential against the freezing cold winters in northern Europe.

A lot of history of the family and castle can be read about in the genealogy room and a visit to the arms room has fine displays of coats-of-arms, weapons and armour. It is a great place to visit for adults and children.

To see all this splendour the opening times are April to September 10am to 6pm, March and October 10am to 5pm and November to February 10am to 4pm. Admission prices are €6 for adults, €4.50 students, €5 senior citizens and €2 for children.

Vianden Chairlift

The easiest way to get up the fairly steep hill to the castle is to take the chairlift. The short ten minute ride will afford some stunning views of Vianden town and save your legs at the same time. The chairlift stops at a restaurant just above the castle so be prepared for a short walk down the rough path. It is advisable to wear some decent footwear.

There are single or return tickets available but if you go up in the chairlift and walk down to the castle remember you will have to hike back up the hill to get a ride back down. The most popular method is to get a one-way ticket and visit the castle on the walk back down to the town. A return ticket is €4.90 and a single is €3.60. As you approach the top of the cable car a photo is taken and this can be purchased at an extra cost of €6.50.

Victor Hugo House & Literature Museum

37, rue de la Gare
L-9420 Vianden
Luxembourg
Tel: +352 2687 4088
www.victor-hugo.lu/

Victor Hugo was a famous French novelist and poet and for several months lived in this mansion in Vianden during his exile in 1871. Having spent a few years in Luxembourg as tourist between 1862 and 1865 he decided that he safe in these surroundings so for a brief while made this pretty town his home. There are many personal possessions to be seen in his house as well as paintings and texts to be admired. His most famous works that everyone will be familiar with must be Les Miserables and The Hunchback of Notre Dame.

The museum operated between 1935 and 1998 but closed for a period of restoration and upgrading. The new hi-tech museum opened in 2002 and now visitors can experience the literary wonders of this great author thanks to modern technology.

The Victor Hugo Museum is open daily from 11am to 5pm but it is worth checking the website or calling before you plan a visit as it does close for quite a few holidays. The admission price is €4 for adults and €3.50 for concessions, with various group discounts available. A guided tour is bookable in advance and costs €30 for one hour or €45 for two hours.

Diekirch Brewery Museum

20-22 Rue de Stavelot
L-9284 Diekirch
Luxembourg
Tel: +352 803 023
www.diekirch.cc

Diekirch is world famous for its brewery which was founded in 1873 and by 1900 it had become the biggest brewery in the Grand Duchy. There have been many revamps and mergers over the years and the brewery is now part of InBev, the biggest brewing group in the world.

The museum holds a private collection of breweriana and many of the items are over 100 years old. There is a small shop where fans of the Diekirch brand can buy bottles and beer glasses, posters and other beer related gifts. The Brewery Museum is situated on the first floor of the Diekirch Museum for Historical Vehicles but it is a separate visitor attraction.

The museum is closed on a Monday but open from 10am to 6pm the rest of the week. Admission prices are €6 for adults and €3 for children.

Valley of the Seven Castles

Eisch Valley
Luxembourg

The Eisch Valley or more informally the Valley of the Seven Castles is an area of lush meadows and shady forests close to the border with Belgium. There are many majestic chateaus and castles along the way; some are ruins but some have been restored and are open to the public.

To make the most of these a National Footpath winds its way past seven of these majestic structures, along peaceful paths and through dappled woodland. For hikers and walker the route is about 22 miles long and is a pleasant way to spend a day with friends and a picnic.

For the less energetic or able-bodied the castles can be visited by car and the route takes about an hour starting from Arlon on the Luxembourg/Begium border.

Heading upstream the castles are Mersch, Schoenfels, Hollenfels, Ansembourg Castle, New Castle of Ansembourg, Septfontaines and Koerich Castle.

National Museum of Art & History

Marché-Aux-Poissons
L-2345
Luxembourg City
Tel: +352 4793 301
www.mnha.public.lu

This museum is built over ten different levels with five of these being underground. A chronological journey is followed as visitors ascend floor by floor from through from our prehistoric origins to the latest experiments. There are some fine examples of tombs from the Iron Age and a Roman mosaic of the Muses. This mosaic is a real treasure from the 3rd century and was only discovered in 1995 in the Luxembourg town of Vichten.

There are displays of Roman, Celtic and Medieval coins as well as art collections old and new. The folklore and traditions of Luxembourg are not forgotten and there are exhibitions that cover the 16th century through to the present day.

The modern square, windowless museum building is rather at odds with its neighbours that are built in the more typical Luxembourg style. The inside is rather maze like but is easy enough to follow and there are information panels in different languages. Access to the different levels is by way of a massive glass lift.

The museum is open Tuesday to Saturday from 10am to 6pm and closed Monday. An adult ticket is €5 and concessions pay €3. Entry is free for children under 18 and disabled visitors. The museum is also open slightly later on a Thursday evening and if you visit between 5pm and 8pm entry is free for everyone. There are quite a few holiday times and other days when the museum might be closed so it is always worth calling before you visit.

Luxembourg Cathedral

Rue Notre-Dame
L-2240
Luxembourg City
Tel: +352 2229 701
www.cathol.lu/

The Cathedral of Luxembourg is nowhere near as big as its French namesake but more than compensates by being a stunning building in its own right. The late Gothic structure was constructed between 1613 and 1621 and enlarged in the 1930's. The 20th century makeover added the tall, narrow spires and new choir stalls and gave the cathedral some rather modern sculptures to contrast with the rather fine Renaissance ornaments and decorations already in situ.

The cathedral is the final resting place of several members of the Grand Ducal family and the entrance to their crypt is closely guarded by two lions, the work of Auguste Trémont. There is an immediate sense of peace and tranquility when you enter the cathedral and the sheer beauty of the interior of this building mustn't be missed.

The cathedral is open from 10am to noon and 2pm to 5.30 pm daily and entrance is free.

Palace of the Grand Dukes

17, rue du Marché-aux-Herbes
L-1728
Luxembourg City

The palace has the most beautiful façade but there is not much outside to give visitors a clue as to the real purpose of the building. There are flags flying and a guard outside the door but many people walk right past without a second glance.

This 16th century Flemish Renaissance building is in fact the official city residence of the Grand Duke. Visiting dignitaries and heads of state from other countries can stay in extensive staterooms on the first floor and many banquets and formal receptions are held in these magnificent surroundings. One of the major events of each year is the New Year's Eve reception for government members and the Chamber of Deputies.

The building was constructed between 1572 and 1574 to be used as the town hall and for 200 years served its purpose admirably. In 1890 major renovations took place, a new wing was added and the Royal Duke and his family moved in. All was well until World War II when the palace was occupied by the Nazis. A lot of damage was done as officers turned this once beautiful building into a concert hall and tavern and many treasures were stolen. The palace has now been restored but the work has taken nearly fifty years.

The rooms are absolutely stunning and have to be seen to be believed but there are tours through some parts of the Grand Ducal Palace in the summer months when the royal family are away. More information is available from the tourist office or go in to the office in person to reserve tickets.

Tickets are €7 euros for adults and €3.50 euros for children. All proceeds go to the "Fondation Grand Duke Henri and Grand Duchess Maria-Teresa."

Les Thermes Water Park

Rue des Thermes
L-8018 Strassen
Luxembourg
Tel: +352 2703 0027
www.lesthermes.net

Luxembourg might be separated from the sea by neighbouring Belgium but if you need to feel the sand between your toes go to Les Thermes Water Park. With over 3,000 square feet of watery fun, beach volleyball and spacious gardens with sun-loungers it will be hard to imagine you are 150 miles from the sea.

For water babies Aqua World at Les Thermes has giant slides, wave pools and children's pools as well as an Olympic size swimming pool. For the less aquatic there are saunas, solariums, a gym and fitness centre and a beauty parlour for some relaxing treatments. In the sauna area there is an ice fountain to cool you down and adventure showers as well as a plunge pool and Jacuzzi. The sauna and steam room area is very traditional and guests are requested to enter and leave in the nude.

There is no need to leave to find something to eat or drink as there are two restaurants in the complex serving up a variety of nutritious snacks and meals. There is a daily special for €10 which includes coffee or with a dessert the price is €12.

The admission prices are varied depending on the facility you wish to use and for how long but there is a comprehensive list on the website. As a guide use of Aqua World for a couple of hours is €6.50 for adults and €3.50 for children. Opening hours are generally between 9am and 9pm every day with some facilities opening slightly earlier.

Luxembourg American Cemetery Memorial

Val du Scheid,
Luxembourg City, L-2517
Tel: +352 431 727
www.abmc.gov/

The Luxembourg American Cemetery and Memorial is in a beautiful wooded area a few miles from the city centre. The 50 acres of lawn with their memorials and graves are immaculately kept and there is an immediate sense of peace and tranquility. The land was granted by the Grand Ducal in 1944 for use as a cemetery without charge in perpetuity.

The gently sloping burial ground is the resting place of 5,076 military dead, many who lost their lives in the advance to the Rhine River and the Battle of the Bulge. Luxembourg was headquarters to General George Patton and he is buried here, facing his men.

If you need help there is always a member of staff on duty who will assist you but there is plenty of helpful information available to help navigate round the cemetery.

The cemetery is open daily from 9am to 5pm except for Christmas Day and New Year's Day.

Recommendations for the Budget Traveller

Places to Stay

Luxembourg City Hostel

2, rue du Fort Olisy
L-2261 Luxembourg City
Tel: +352 262 766 650
www.youthhostels.lu

The Luxembourg City Hostel is a great place to stay for families, friends and individuals. The hostel is centrally located so access to all the fabulous attractions of Luxembourg City centre are close at hand. There are excellent transport links close by as well as many shop, bars and restaurants.

This modern hostel has internet access, a bicycle storeroom, conference rooms and a parking space for coaches. There is a cafeteria that offers food and drinks all day; with Luxembourgish specialities on the menu as well as vegetarian meals, barbeques and buffets. Group menus can be catered for by prior arrangement.

Luxembourg City Hostel is open all year round and guests of all ages are welcome as well as disabled travellers. The reception is open 24 hours a day and the friendly, welcoming staff will do their best to help guests out however they can. A bed for a night in a shared room costs from €21.

Il Piccolo Mondo

216, rue de Hamm
L-1713 Luxembourg
Tel: +352 428 661
www.piccolomondo.lu/

This small hotel is a few kilometres away from the city centre and the airport but there is a bus stop outside which connects with the main train station and the town centre.

The hotel has 12 rooms with a choice of one, two or three beds. All the rooms have private bathrooms as well as flat screen TV, a hairdryer and heating. There is free Wifi and a continental breakfast included in the price. The prices start at €50 for a single room up to €70 for three beds depending on the time of the year.

Il Piccolo Mondo is also a restaurant-pizzeria and a variety of Italian cuisine is served including speciality pizzas from the wood-fired ovens. For sunny days there is a terrace where guests can enjoy meals outside. At lunchtime on weekdays there is a fixed price menu available for just €10.

Ibis Budget Hotel, Luxembourg Airport

Route de Trèves,
L-2632 Luxembourg
Tel: +352 422 613 10
www.ibis.com/

This is a great hotel for travellers on a budget who are looking for simple accommodation with no frills. The rooms have one double and two single beds so are great for family or friends to share. All the rooms have private bathrooms, air-conditioning and free Wifi access.
There is a substantial continental buffet style breakfast with cold meats, locally produced breads and croissants, cereals, toast and preserves for a small extra cost.

The room price starts at €49 depending on the season and there are occasionally special offers for early bookings or for certain dates. The hotel is very close to Luxembourg's Findel Airport and there is a free shuttle service between the two.

Hotel Parc Belle-Vue

5, Avenue Marie Therese
L-2132 Luxembourg City
Tel: +352 456 1411
www.parcbellevue.lu/

Hotel Parc Belle-Vue has an enviable setting; it is almost surrounded by lush greenery yet only a few minutes' walk from the city centre of Luxembourg.

There are 54 Comfort rooms and 5 Superior rooms all with twin beds and all decorated in contemporary style with top quality furniture, soft furnishings and bedding. All of the rooms have private bathrooms and are equipped with a desk, hairdryer, satellite television and a safe. There is a laundry service and dogs are welcome. The price per room is around €100 but special offers are available online.

Le Bec Fin restaurant is a favourite with the locals and there is daily hot and cold buffet as well as a wide selection of daily specials. Barbeques are held on the large terrace where guests can admire the views across the park. Le Bateau Ivre bar is similar to an English pub where international guests can meet for a few drinks and take part in an old-fashioned game of skittles while they exchange experiences.

Il Castello Borghese

86 route de Trèves
L-2633 Senningerberg
Luxembourg
Tel: +352 349 001
www.castelloborghese.lu/

Il Castello Borghese is in the small pretty town of
Senningberg on the edge of the Grengewald forest and it
is perfect for rest and relaxation but still close to the major
attractions. The capital is around a 15 minute drive away
and there are excellent road connections to the city and
the nearby airport.

The hotel is small but there is a choice of single and
double rooms as well as four bedded family rooms. Prices
for a single room start at €37 up to €78 for the quadruple
room and that includes continental breakfast. The
functional rooms are all smartly decorated and all have
private bathrooms, free Wifi, a desk and TV with satellite
channels.

There is a lovely restaurant that serves French and Italian
cuisine and guests can enjoy meals and drinks on the
terrace in the summer months. It is a very popular spot
with the locals who come to take advantage of the large
pizzas and excellent range of pasta dishes.

Places to Eat & Drink

La Fontaine

25, place de Paris
L-2314 Luxembourg City
Tel +352 494 076

Luxembourg is full of expensive places to eat but La Fontaine offers daily specials from €8. It is easy to find between the old city and the station and is not far from Petrusse Valley Park.

The restaurant has menus in four languages so you can be sure you are ordering something you like. One of the Luxembourgish classic dishes is smoked pork neck with broad beans but if you don't fancy that there is a wide choice from mussels to pizzas. La Fontaine is open seven days a week.

Mousel Cantine

46, Montée de Clausen
L-1343 Luxembourg City
Tel: +352 470 198
www.mouselscantine.lu/

Luxembourg has many specialties when it comes to food and in Mousel Cantine there is a wide choice. Take some time to find this restaurant in the heart of the Grund, a warren of narrow streets on the banks of the Alzette River, and try a tender grilled pork knuckle, or some braised pigs trotters or beef tenderloin with an accompaniment of sauerkraut. For the adventurous types there is horsemeat served with garlic sauce. The portions are huge and go down easily with a few tankards of Mousel beer.

The starters are priced from €5 and the main courses from €14.50 with a good selection of salads and entrees as well. There is a daily special and a children's menu plus some calorie-laden deserts. Mousel Cantine is open all day every day, apart from Saturday lunchtime and closed on a Sunday.

A La Soupe

9 Rue Chimay
L-1333 Luxembourg City
Tel: +352 2620 2047
www.alasoupe.net

A La Soupe is an unusual café and as the name implies
the menu is based on soups. There are classic soups as
well as a wide variety of sweet and savoury flavours. This
smart café has a steady local clientele who come to enjoy
the healthy alternatives to fast food on offer. All the soups
are produced with special care from locally grown,
seasonal produce.

A daily menu is available and costs €10 and includes a
soup or salad and dessert with a hot drink or a cold soft
drink. For early risers there is a selection of breakfast
items on the menu from 8.30 am to 11am with a choice of
toast, cereals, cakes, fruit salad and cheeses with fair trade
coffee and a range of organic teas.

A La Soupe is open from 7am to 8.30 pm every day except
Sunday. For anyone who is interested in learning more
about how the chefs prepare these nutritious soups the
restaurant has cooking classes. For a very reasonable €15
an afternoon can be spent at A La Soupe and adults and
children are welcome.

Bistrot de la Presse

24 Rue de Marché aux Herbes
L-1728 Luxembourg City
Tel: + 352 466 6669
www.bistrotdelapresse.lu/

Bistrot de la Presse is very close to Luxembourg Cathedral and is an ideal place for a meal before or after a visit to this beautiful 17th century Gothic structure. The restaurant is in the elegant Rue de Marché aux Herbes and diners can enjoy the ambience of Luxembourg City from the pretty terrace.

The daily special costs €12 but there is an á la carte menu to choose from with delicious sounding salads, hams and cheeses. One of the most popular dishes is a hearty and warming tureen of bouneschlupp (green bean soup with sausage) and with some crusty bread it is a meal in itself. Half a litre of a decent wine to wash it down with is around €6.

Bistrot de la Presse is open Monday to Friday 7.30am until midnight and Saturday 9.00am to midnight, closed on Sunday. The staff speak six different languages between them including English so there are no problems in being understood.

La Table du Pain

37 Ave de la Liberté
L-1931 Luxembourg City
Tel: +352 295 663

Av. Monterey 19
L-2163 Luxembourg City
Tel: +352 241 608
www.tabledupain.lu

La Table du Pain is a small bakery chain with two cafés in the centre of Luxembourg. The Ave de la Liberté branch is close to the main train station and the one in Avenue Monterey is not far from the Place d'Armes and the old town area. Both shops are open all day every day from 7am to 7pm.

There is a decent selection of soups, salads and sandwiches on offer along with hot meals and a daily special. The locals frequent La Table du Pain for breakfast and coffee and can be seen taking home freshly baked loaves and boxes of melt in your mouth pastries and cakes. If you are stuck for ideas as to what to put on your bagels and breads there is a range of jellies and jams on sale.

Places to Shop

Place Guillaume Market

Place Guillaume II
L-1648 Luxembourg City

Place Guillame II is affectionately known as the "Knuedler" and on a Wednesday and Saturday plays host to the local produce market. This busy square is a mass of brightly coloured stalls selling locally grown fresh fruit and vegetables; home cured hams and freshly baked breads.

There are dairy products, fresh fish stalls, flower stalls and much more all vying for your custom under the watchful eye of a bronze statue of King and Duke William XI of Nassau-Orange. The market takes place at Place Guillame II and also at the nearby Place de Paris and is open both days from 7.30am to 1pm.

Centre Commercial Auchan

5 rue Alphonse Weicker
L-2721 Luxembourg
Tel: +352 437 7431
www.auchan.lu/

The 40,000 square feet of the Auchan shopping centre is a few miles away from Luxembourg City centre but access is great by car or bus.

There is plenty of underground parking and next door to this giant retail therapy paradise there is a huge multi-screen cinema complex.

The shops are spread over two floors with the food and drinks on level 0 and the clothes shops and household stores on level 1. If you need to take a break from all the bright lights and jingling tills there are about 20 different places to eat and drink; choose from pizzerias, soup bars, cafeterias, oriental restaurants and much, much more.

Auchan is open Monday to Saturday from 8am to 8pm and closes one hour later at 9pm on a Friday. If you want bulk shopping of drinks, pet food, compost or coal and household goods like detergents there are over 100 products available through the innovative Drink Shop. Simply drive down to the basement, place your order and it is loaded into the car for you.

Flea Market

Place d'Armes
L-2633 Luxembourg City

If you are in Luxembourg on the second or fourth Saturday of the month head for Place d'Armes and see if there are any treasures to be found in among the second-hand items, antiques and collectibles. From 9am to 2pm locals and visitors flock to the square that long ago was used as a parade ground for the troops.

In the summer months the parasols from the numerous bars and cafes make a bright splash of colour across the square and the central bandstand presents concerts from local and visiting groups.

Mexx

30, Grand-Rue
L-1660 Luxembourg City
Tel: +352 2673 8830
www.mexx.com

Mexx is a Dutch brand that launched itself into the world of fashion in the early 1980's. The original idea came from collections designed by an Indian born Dutch businessman Kul Rattan Chadha in the 1970's and today there are 65 shops worldwide.

Originally designed for men and women the collections have expanded to include children's wear, clothing accessories, perfumes and textiles for the home. The Luxembourg City centre flagship store is open Monday to Thursday 10am to 6pm and Friday and Saturday 9.30am to 6.30pm.

Namur Chocolatier

44, av. de la Liberté
L-1930 Luxembourg City
Tel.: +352 493 964
www.namur.lu

For visitors to Luxembourg with a sweet tooth Namur Chocolatier has to be the place to go. There are many high-end chocolate shops in Luxembourg but Namur is a national institution.

The founder Nicolas Namur headed for the bright lights of New York in 1851 but returned in 1893 to his birthplace to open his first patisserie. There are several branches of Namur in and around the city, including the bigger production centre at Hamm.

The master confectioners use recipes that have been passed down through the generations as well as creating new more modern flavoured sweets and pastries. Only the finest ingredients are good enough; senga-sengana strawberries, Turin chestnuts, Sicilian almonds and untreated oranges from Seville are just a few of the carefully selected products used.

The chocolates are made in small quantities to ensure freshness and the pastries are made daily. There are Luxembourgish specialties such as Luxemburgli (macaroons) and Baamkuch (a layered cake) as well as chocolate cakes, Bavarian pies and many, many more delights to choose from.

Namur Chocolatier on av. de la Liberté is only a few minutes' walk from the main train station and is open Monday 12 noon to 6pm and Tuesday to Saturday 7.45am to 6pm.

Printed in Great Britain
by Amazon